Mothers and Daughters

THE SPECIAL BOND BETWEEN US

EDITED BY SARAH ARAK

Introduction

THERE IS A MAGICAL MOMENT IN TIME WHEN THE RELATIONSHIP between mother and daughter transforms from that of parent-child to one of equals. The daughter is no longer viewed as a helpless child struggling to apply lipstick and walk in high heels without teetering; and the mother is no longer viewed as the disciplinarian policing a ten o'clock curfew. Rather, both view each other as confidants, allies, and best friends.

The bond between mothers and daughters is unlike any other experience two women will share in their lifetimes. It will constantly evolve and strengthen as they grow older. Its roots run deeper than any other familial bond, in part because mothers and daughters (while they might not want to admit it) are so very much alike. No other relationship will come close to rivaling the deep, intuitive, emotional bond that exists between them.

While no mother-daughter relationship is perfect, each is characterized by a unique connection that requires very little explicit communication. The slightest gesture, sigh, or tone of voice is enough to convey entire paragraphs of information. And while it's difficult to put this connection into words, it's important now and then to express how very special that bond is.

A DAUGHTER IS A MOTHER'S GENDER PARTNER,

HER CLOSEST ALLY IN THE FAMILY CONFEDERACY,

AN EXTENSION OF HER SELF.

—Victoria Secunda

SHE TRIED IN EVERY WAY TO UNDERSTAND ME,

AND SHE SUCCEEDED. IT WAS THIS DEEP,

LOVING UNDERSTANDING AS LONG AS SHE LIVED,

MORE THAN ANYTHING ELSE, THAT HELPED AND

SUSTAINED ME ON MY WAY TO SUCCESS.

—Mae West

My mother is a poem

I'll never be able to write,

though everything I write

is a poem to my mother.

—Sharon Doubiago

A MOTHER'S LOVE IS PATIENT AND FORGIVING,

WHEN ALL OTHERS ARE FORSAKING;

AND IT NEVER FAILS OR FALTERS,

EVEN WHEN THE HEART IS BREAKING.

—Helen Steiner Rice

THERE IS A POINT AT WHICH YOU AREN'T

AS MUCH MOM AND DAUGHTER AS

YOU ARE ADULTS AND FRIENDS.

—Jamie Lee Curtis

OUR MOTHERS AND GRANDMOTHERS HAVE,

MORE OFTEN THAN NOT ANONYMOUSLY,

HANDED ON THE CREATIVE SPARK, THE SEED OF THE

FLOWER THEY THEMSELVES NEVER HOPED TO SEE—OR LIKE

A SEALED LETTER THEY COULD NOT PLAINLY READ.

—Alice Walker

WHAT I WOULD LIKE TO GIVE MY DAUGHTER

IS FREEDOM. AND THIS IS SOMETHING THAT MUST BE

GIVEN BY EXAMPLE, NOT BY EXHORTATION. FREEDOM IS

A LOOSE LEASH, A LICENSE TO BE DIFFERENT FROM

YOUR MOTHER AND STILL BE LOVED.

—Erica Jong

Thou art thy mother's glass, and she in thee,

Calls back the lovely April of her prime.

— William Shakespeare

A MOTHER GIVES HER DAUGHTER

HER WINGS BY GIVING HER THE SELF-CONFIDENCE

TO MAKE HER OWN DECISIONS.

—Priscilla Presley

UNLIKE THE MOTHER-SON RELATIONSHIP,

A DAUGHTER'S RELATIONSHIP WITH HER MOTHER

IS SOMETHING AKIN TO BUNGEE DIVING. SHE CAN STAKE

HER CLAIM IN THE OUTSIDE WORLD—BUT THERE IS

AN INVISIBLE EMOTIONAL CORD THAT SNAPS HER BACK.

—Victoria Secunda

THERE IS NO INFLUENCE SO POWERFUL

AS THAT OF THE MOTHER.

—Sarah Josepha Hale

A MOTHER LAUGHS OUR LAUGHTER,

SHEDS OUR TEARS,

RETURNS OUR LOVE,

FEARS OUR FEARS.

SHE LIVES OUR JOYS,

CARES OUR CARES,

AND ALL OUR HOPES AND DREAMS SHE SHARES.

—Julia Summers

A DAUGHTER REMINDS YOU OF ALL

THE THINGS YOU HAD FORGOTTEN

ABOUT BEING YOUNG.

—Maeve O'Reilly

MOST OF ALL THE OTHER BEAUTIFUL THINGS

IN LIFE COME BY TWOS AND THREES, BY DOZENS

AND HUNDREDS. PLENTY OF ROSES, STARS, SUNSETS,

RAINBOWS, BROTHERS AND SISTERS, AUNTS AND

COUSINS, COMRADES AND FRIENDS; BUT ONLY

ONE MOTHER IN THE WHOLE WORLD.

—Kate Douglas Wiggin

WHO RAN TO HELP ME WHEN I FELL,

AND WOULD SOME PRETTY STORY TELL,

OR KISS THE PLACE TO MAKE IT WELL?

MY MOTHER.

— Ann Taylor

CHANCE MADE YOU MY DAUGHTER;

LOVE MADE YOU MY FRIEND.

—Author Unknown

NEVER GROW A WISHBONE, DAUGHTER,

WHERE YOUR BACKBONE OUGHT TO BE.

—Clementine Paddleford

WHEN I STOPPED SEEING MY MOTHER

WITH THE EYES OF A CHILD,

I SAW THE WOMAN WHO HELPED ME

GIVE BIRTH TO MYSELF.

—Nancy Friday

A MOTHER IS THE ONE TO WHOM YOU HURRY

WHEN YOU ARE TROUBLED.

—Emily Dickinson

SOME MOTHERS ARE KISSING MOTHERS AND

SOME ARE SCOLDING MOTHERS, BUT IT IS LOVE

JUST THE SAME, AND MOST MOTHERS

KISS AND SCOLD TOGETHER.

—Pearl S. Buck

BEING A FULL-TIME MOTHER IS ONE

OF THE HIGHEST SALARIED JOBS IN MY FIELD,

SINCE THE PAYMENT IS PURE LOVE.

—Mildred B. Vermont

A MOTHER IS THE TRUEST FRIEND WE HAVE,

WHEN TRIALS, HEAVY AND SUDDEN, FALL UPON US...

STILL WILL SHE CLING TO US, AND ENDEAVOR BY

HER KIND PRECEPTS AND COUNSELS TO DISSIPATE

THE CLOUDS OF DARKNESS, AND CAUSE

PEACE TO RETURN TO OUR HEARTS.

—Washington Irving

IT WAS MY MOTHER WHO GAVE ME MY VOICE.

SHE DID THIS, I KNOW NOW, BY CLEARING A SPACE

WHERE MY WORDS COULD FALL, GROW,

THEN FIND THEIR WAY TO OTHERS.

—Paula Giddings

THE ROLE OF MOTHER IS PROBABLY

THE MOST IMPORTANT CAREER

A WOMAN CAN HAVE.

—Janet Mary Riley

MOTHERS OF DAUGHTERS ARE DAUGHTERS

OF MOTHERS AND HAVE REMAINED SO, IN CIRCLES

JOINED TO CIRCLES, SINCE TIME BEGAN.

—Signe Hammer

A MOTHER'S TREASURE IS HER DAUGHTER.

— Catherine Pulsifer

LIFE WITH A DAUGHTER IS A SPECIAL

EXPERIENCE FOR PARENTS, PARTICULARLY MOTHERS.

YOU ARE FAR ENOUGH AWAY TO HAVE SOME

PERSPECTIVE ON WHAT YOUR DAUGHTER IS

GOING THROUGH. STILL, YOU ARE CLOSE ENOUGH,

IF REMINDED, TO FEEL IT ALL AGAIN.

—Stella Chess

THE HEART OF A MOTHER IS A

DEEP ABYSS AT THE BOTTOM OF WHICH YOU

WILL ALWAYS FIND FORGIVENESS.

—Honoré de Balzac

YOU NEVER REALIZE HOW MUCH YOUR MOTHER LOVES YOU

TILL YOU EXPLORE THE ATTIC—AND FIND EVERY LETTER

YOU EVER SENT HER, EVERY FINGER PAINTING,

CLAY POT, BEAD NECKLACE, EASTER CHICKEN, CARDBOARD

SANTA CLAUS, PAPERLACE MOTHER'S DAY CARD

AND SCHOOL REPORT SINCE DAY ONE.

—Pam Brown

A MOTHER'S ARMS ARE MADE OF

TENDERNESS, AND CHILDREN

SLEEP SOUNDLY IN THEM.

—Victor Hugo

As a child, you never quite understood

how your mom was able to know exactly

what you were thinking... Sometimes Mom would

know what you were thinking before the

thought even entered into your head.

—Linda Sunshine

THE MOTHER IS ONLY REALLY THE MISTRESS

OF HER DAUGHTER UPON THE CONDITION OF

CONTINUALLY REPRESENTING HERSELF

TO HER AS A MODEL OF WISDOM.

—Alexandre Dumas Père

MY MOTHER DREW A DISTINCTION BETWEEN ACHIEVEMENT AND SUCCESS. SHE SAID: 'ACHIEVEMENT IS THE KNOWLEDGE THAT YOU HAVE STUDIED, WORKED HARD AND DONE THE BEST THAT IS IN YOU. SUCCESS IS BEING PRAISED BY OTHERS, AND THAT'S NICE, TOO, BUT NOT AS IMPORTANT OR AS SATISFYING.'

—Helen Hayes

THE DAUGHTER NEVER EVER GIVES UP
ON THE MOTHER, JUST AS THE MOTHER NEVER
GIVES UP ON THE DAUGHTER. THERE IS A TIE
THERE SO STRONG THAT NOTHING CAN BREAK IT.

—Rachel Billington

ALL WOMEN BECOME LIKE THEIR MOTHERS.

THAT IS THEIR TRAGEDY.

NO MAN DOES. THAT'S HIS.

—Oscar Wilde

THE PRECURSOR OF THE MIRROR

IS THE MOTHER'S FACE.

—D. W. Winnicott

THE MOTHER SHOULD TEACH HER

DAUGHTER ABOVE ALL THINGS

TO KNOW HERSELF.

—C. E. Sargent

MOTHERS, LOOK AFTER YOUR DAUGHTERS,

KEEP THEM NEAR YOU, KEEP THEIR CONFIDENCE—

THAT THEY MAY BE TRUE AND FAITHFUL.

—Elmina S. Taylor

BIOLOGY IS THE LEAST OF WHAT

MAKES SOMEONE A MOTHER.

—Oprah Winfrey

BELOVED, YOU ARE MY SISTER,

YOU ARE MY DAUGHTER,

YOU ARE MY FACE; YOU ARE ME.

—Toni Morrison

WE ONLY HAVE ONE MOM, ONE MOMMY,

ONE MOTHER IN THIS WORLD.

DON'T WAIT FOR THE TOMORROW

TO TELL MOM YOU LOVE HER.

—Author Unknown

DAUGHTER, THERE ARE NOT ENOUGH WORDS

TO TELL YOU HOW MUCH I LOVE YOU!

—Catherine Pulsifer

PHOTO CREDITS

COVER PHOTO: entropy; P. 4: Elea Dumas; P. 6: Tanya Constantine; P. 8: Ibid; P. 10: Ibid; P. 12: Gary Moss; P. 14: Plush Studios; P. 16: Plush Studios; P. 18: Ibid; P. 20: ER Productions; P. 22: Simon Watson; P. 24: Don Carstens; P. 26: Ibid; P. 28: Maria Taglienti-Molinari; P. 30: Ibid; P. 32: Tanya Constantine; P. 34: Macduff Everton; P. 36: Ibid; P. 38: Burke/Triolo Productions; P. 40: Elea Dumas; P. 42: Val Loh; P. 44: entropy; P. 46: Eleonora Ghioldi; P. 48: Ibid; P. 50: Tanya Constantine; P. 52: Elisa Cicinelli; P. 54: Paula Hible; P. 56: Christina Kennedy; P. 58: Jack Hollingsworth; P. 60: Ibid; P. 62: Elyse Lewin; P. 64: Ibid; P. 66: Ibid; P. 68: Southern Stock; P. 70: SW Productions; P. 72: Lilly Dong; P. 74: Heather Weston; P. 76: Simon Watson; P. 78: Southern Stock; P. 80: entropy; P. 82: Val Loh; P. 85: Ibid; P. 86: Melanie Acevedo.

The beautiful photos you see throughout this book are courtesy of Jupiterimages.
For more information on the contributing photographers, visit www.jupiterimages.com.

jupiterimages.